HAPPY KIDS' HANDBOOK

Empowering Children's Self-Esteem, building a Growth Mindset, and cultivating Emotionally Intelligent Kids.

CARRIE KHANG

FREE BONUS

7 pages Mindset Printable

4 pages Motivational Poster Printable

Get Our Next Book for Free

TABLE OF CONTENTS

1. Be Confident, Be You..p.1

2. Kindness Rocks: Fill, Share, and Shine!......................p.12

3. The Emotion Toolbox..p.20

4. Rise and Shine with Confidence................................p.31

5. Think Big, Grow Bigger..p.39

6. Friendship Explorer's Handbook...............................p.46

7. Superpower Habits...p.54

8. Magical Manners..p.61

Conclusion...p.71

INTRODUCTION

Are you ready to become the most awesome version of yourself? This book will help you discover your hidden powers and unleash your inner superhero! You're great already, but we're here to help you to get rid of all those worries and feel fantastic about yourself.

You might feel like you're on a rollercoaster, but the ride will be worth it once you find out what your special abilities are. You'll be surprised by how much more you can do and how truly amazing you can become!

Excited to get to know the smarter, stronger, happier, and totally incredible YOU? Of course you are!

You'll learn lots of cool stuff in this book. We'll teach you things like positive self-talk (that means being nice to yourself) and controlling your emotions. We'll also talk about building confidence and developing a growth mindset. You'll also learn how to be a great friend and have good money habits. Plus, there's a whole lot more!

So put on your superhero cape (or maybe just your comfiest PJs), buckle up, and brace yourself for a wild ride filled with fun, laughter, and tons of exciting challenges.

You've got what it takes to be that inspiring, extraordinary kid that shines like a diamond. No kidding! Let's dive in and discover all the wonderful things you're capable of!

1

BE CONFIDENT, BE YOU

hen you look in the mirror, what do you see? What sorts of things do you say about your appearance?

In the famous story The Ugly Duckling, there was a duckling who did not look like his brothers and sisters. He was too big and had dark feathers. He was different, so he was called ugly. Because of this, other animals laughed at him and pushed him away. But later on, he saw his reflection in the water and was surprised to find that he had grown into a beautiful and graceful swan.

Do you sometimes feel like this duckling, like you don't belong with the other children? Are there times when they make fun of you because you're different in some way?

Don't worry. You're not alone. A lot of children like you experience the same thing. They also feel ugly at times. There are moments when they also feel like they are not good enough.

Maybe someone said your eyes are too big. Or that your skin is dark.

Maybe sports are hard for you. Or you don't dress in popular styles like other kids.

Maybe you're not very good at math or spelling. Or you can't sing so well.

That's okay! We are all born different from one another. We were all made to be unique, with our own bodies and our own set of talents.

The Ugly Duckling later turned out to be a lovely swan. As you get older, you too will soon discover what's so awesome about you!

What's Amazing About You?

It's all right to feel bad about ourselves sometimes. It happens to everybody.

Many people, even adults, are not aware of their wonderful qualities unless others point them out. But the truth is, we are all special! We all have hidden treasures that we might not know about yet. They are inside us, waiting to be discovered!

Now look at yourself in the mirror again. Remember that you look good in your own way. You don't have to look like other kids to look good.

Smile at yourself. Complete these sentences:

"I love myself because _____."

"I am good at _____."

"I am proud of myself because _____."

"I feel good when people say _____."

It does not have to be something big. It can be small or simple, such as the following:

"I love myself because I'm always curious, and I love learning new things."

"I am good at listening to my teacher and obeying my parents."

"I am proud of myself because I share my snacks with my classmates."

"I feel good when people say I make them laugh."

Try it out. Bet you can think of a lot more!

When you focus your mind on the good things, you'll discover just how awesome you really are. And even if they are little, everyday things, they can pile up and show you what cool stuff you're truly made of!

. . .

Don't Say Negative Things About Yourself

Did you know that plants can grow tall when we say nice words to them?

Yep, that's right! It sounds silly, but several experiments show it's true. When you say "You're so beautiful" to a plant while watering it, it grows bigger and faster, and it blooms magnificently!

But if you say "I hate you" and "You're really ugly" to a plant, it certainly won't grow and flourish in the same way. It's likely to dry up or refuse to blossom.

Words are very powerful. That's why saying positive words to yourself is important!

Just like plants, you also need kind words. That includes saying nice things to yourself. If you tell yourself "I'm amazing!", then you'll feel great. You'll probably feel like you can do just about anything and have fun too. But if you keep saying "I'm stupid" and "I can't do it", then you'll feel so down you won't get to do anything else but mope around.

Next time you feel bad about something you can't do yet, try using the power of the word "yet." Add "yet" at the end of a sentence when you say you can't do something. For example, you can say, "I'm not good at riding a bike yet" or "I can't paint well yet." It will remind you that you're still learning. Your other skills and talents may come out later.

I DON'T UNDERSTAND THIS...

I CAN'T DO THIS...

I'M NOT GOOD AT THIS...

IT DOESN'T WORK...

THIS DOESN'T MAKE SENSE...

Starting today, stop describing yourself as "not smart" or "not having friends" or "not as good-looking as him." Instead, think of what makes you wonderful and special in your own way.

How did you make your Mom, Dad, or another family member smile last? Maybe you said something funny. Now that's something great about you!

Think about when a classmate wanted to hang out with you. Maybe you helped him with his homework. Now that's something else you can be proud of!

Keep saying these nice things to yourself. Soon, you will grow tall and strong like a tree. You will blossom like a beautiful flower. It's only a matter of time.

Don't Compare Yourself to Others

Have you ever seen a caterpillar? Some say a caterpillar is a weird-looking creature with a long body and lots of legs. Not really what you'd call "beautiful." It just munches on leaves and crawls around all day. Do you want to look like a caterpillar? I don't think so.

But do you know what's great about caterpillars? They all eventually turn into pretty butterflies. That's when they can spread their colorful wings and fly in the air.

We all start out as caterpillars. Some turn to butterflies earlier than others. So don't be sad and afraid. If you are not good at some things yet, it's only temporary. And if you may not look a certain way, remember that you are still young and many changes will happen to your body as you grow up.

Now think about this. How does it make you feel when your friend can solve a puzzle that you keep getting stuck on? Do you feel sad when your brother or sister gets compliments for getting high grades in school?

It's okay to admit how you feel about such things. Maybe your sibling is more advanced in some ways. But you're better at other things.

Perhaps you're great at organizing things, and your friend wishes they could be like you because of this. Your siblings may get higher grades than you, but they could also want to be good singers or dancers like you.

Focus on what you have and what you can do. Let these wonderful things shine! Be proud and happy about these things you can do. Some other people can't do those yet.

You are great in your own way. Smile and know that you are learning, growing, and becoming the best you can be.

Positive Self-Talk

Hey, want to know the secret to feeling confident and happy all the time?

Make that inner voice in your head your best-best-BEST friend!

Yup, that's right. But how do you do that? By teaching your inner voice always to say something positive wherever you go and whatever you do.

Let's say your best friend falls while learning to roller skate. Is it nice to laugh at him and say, "You're so stupid! You'll never be able to learn how to skate!"? Of course not! So it's the same when you make a mistake or fail at something. You must remember to be kind to yourself just like you would to a friend. Give yourself a pat on the back and say, "You tried your best today. Good job! Just keep practicing, and you'll get better and better."

Positive self-talk means being your own cheerleader. It means smiling and making yourself feel good with the words in your mind.

You can make speaking nicely to yourself a habit. Just practice it every day. When you do that, the positive words will soon come even when you're not thinking about it.

The next time you feel bad about something, your inner voice will not say, "I told you so!" or "You're so dumb!" Instead, it's going to remind you, "Everyone makes mistakes. You can get up and try again."

Talk to yourself the way you talk to your best friend. Try saying the following things to yourself and see how they make you feel:

"I believe in myself."

"I am brave and strong."

"I can learn from my mistakes and grow."

"It's okay not to be perfect."

"I can forgive myself and try again."

"It's normal to feel this way, and I can get through it."

"I treat myself with kindness."

"I still deserve love and kindness even if I make mistakes."

"I can be my own best friend."

Are you starting to feel happier and more confident in yourself? This is just the beginning. You're doing great! Just keep it up!

SELF- ESTEEM COPING STATEMENTS

I AM ENOUGH

I AM CAPABLE

I AM WORTHY OF LOVE

I CAN TAKE CARE OF MYSELF

I AM IN CHARGE OF MY DESTINY

IT'S OK TO MAKE MISTAKES

I AM BEAUTIFUL

I CAN DO HARD THINGS

I MAKE PEOPLE SMILE

I AM SO LOVED

I AM A GOOD PERSON

I BELIEVE IN ME

TODAY IS MY DAY !

2

KINDNESS ROCKS: FILL, SHARE, AND SHINE!

I magine that you're carrying an invisible bucket. It's not filled with water but with good thoughts and good feelings. The bucket is a symbol of our positive thoughts and feelings.

Everyone in the world starts out with an invisible bucket. You have a bucket. Your best friend has one too. Your parents have their own buckets. Your brothers and sisters all have the same buckets too.

If all of us have this invisible bucket of goodness and happiness, then shouldn't we all be happy?

Sometimes, we are not happy because the bucket isn't filled. Maybe it's half-filled. At times, it's even empty. And that's when we get feelings that don't feel good. We can feel sad, lonely, afraid, frustrated, and worried.

When the Bucket is Full

When your bucket is full, you are filled with wonderful thoughts and awesome feelings.

It makes you want to cheer up your best friend or play with your little brothers and sisters. When someone teases you or accidentally hurts you, you don't make a big deal out of it — because your bucket is full.

When it is full, you're super happy! You feel great, as if you could fly in the sky!

Many times, when this happens, you may feel like you want to share some of those many good feelings in your bucket. You can make the new kid in school feel welcome. You can help Mom and Dad with the house chores. Helping others feel good makes you feel good, too. You fill their buckets, and they fill yours too.

A full bucket can make you feel joyful, excited, confident, friendly, calm, and loved.

. . .

When the Bucket is Empty

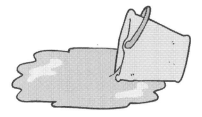

Sometimes, when someone hurts you or makes you feel bad, your bucket does not have so many good feelings. Sometimes it becomes empty.

There are also times when the bucket loses good feelings because of something you did. For example, if you shouted at your friend, it may have made you feel sad and guilty. Shouting may have taken away some of your good feelings from the bucket.

When it comes to something you did, you can take control. You can prevent your bucket from getting empty.

However, there will be experiences that you have no control over. For example, maybe you're super excited to have a picnic at the park, but the entire place turns out to be packed so you can't! Or your classmate says something mean about you, and it makes you feel bad. These things can make you lose the positive thoughts and feelings in your bucket.

An empty bucket can make you feel stressed, depressed, scared, angry, worried, nervous, and sick. You don't want that, do you?

Y ou Can Be in Charge of Your Bucket!

I'm going to let you in on a secret! Here's the good news — even if there are things you cannot control, you can still choose how to react to them. That way, your bucket is not emptied when something happens to you!

Let's say you are having a birthday party outside, but a storm comes. You can just choose to take everyone inside and play indoor games. Your party can still be fun! Instead of crying or getting angry, you can think of the rain as a sign of blessings to come. You can just ask your guests to come in and continue the fun inside.

You can be in charge of your bucket. You can keep filling it up by loving yourself and being kind to yourself.

When you do something you like and enjoy, you're filling your bucket.

When you smile and feel proud of what you have done, you're filling your bucket.

When you positively talk to yourself, you're filling your bucket.

Remember this: You are in charge. You're a champion!

Fill More Buckets Every Day!

Besides filling your bucket, you can help fill other people's buckets too. You can do this by doing good deeds and by spreading kindness.

Kindness is a gift. It involves doing something to make another person feel good. It's about being generous and considerate.

When you say thank you to your teacher for giving you a good lesson or activity, you're being kind and filling your teacher's bucket.

When you help your brother with his school project, you're being kind and filling his bucket.

When you smile at the neighbor and say, "Good Morning!", you're being kind and filling their bucket.

Can you think of other ways that you can fill other people's buckets and make them happy? How else can you show kindness?

Maybe you can sit with the new student at lunch. You can help your friend study for a test if he's having a hard time understanding the lessons. You can even donate your old toys and books or volunteer at an animal shelter! There are lots of ways to fill other people's buckets! I bet you can think of more!

Every single day, wherever you are, picture everyone with their invisible buckets. If you see a classmate frowning, maybe his bucket is not so full today. What can you do to be kind to him? What can you do to cheer him up? Even if your classmate is smiling, it's always great to add more to his bucket.

THE SELF-ESTEEM BUCKET

Wha fills your bucket?

What mends the holes in your bucket?

What causes holes in your bucket?

THE EMOTION TOOLBOX

Have you ever watched the Disney Pixar movie "Inside Out"? In this movie, the characters named Joy, Sadness, Anger, Fear, and Disgust are all emotions that live inside the mind of a young girl named Riley.

Just like Riley, you also have a whole range of emotions inside you that may sometimes feel overwhelming or confusing. Most of the time, you just can't understand them. There are times when you simply want to kick all those feelings out. But of course, you can't. People always have emotions. It's just the way it is!

But there's nothing to worry about! Everybody has confusing emotions sometimes, even adults.

What's important is for us to understand the different emotions that we have inside us. Then we can accept them and manage them better.

ll Feelings Are Okay

The movie characters Joy, Sadness, Anger, Fear, and Disgust are not good or bad, positive or negative. They are just themselves. It's the same with real feelings of people like you. These emotions only turn into something good or bad based on what we do about them or how we react.

All feelings are okay. It's okay to feel sad or angry or scared. It's normal. It happens to everyone. It doesn't make you bad or mean or weak.

When you're always feeling joyful and calm, it also doesn't make you a better person. It's how you use these feelings that can turn them into something good. For example, if you are happy and this makes you see the good in everyone, then that's an amazing feeling!

Who do you consider the kindest person you've ever met? Ask that person if they have gotten angry in the past. Most likely, the answer will be yes. But even though they got angry, it doesn't make them bad. Maybe they still showed good behavior, such as staying calm and forgiving the person that made them mad. They may have gotten angry, but they chose not to get carried away. They chose to react in a positive way.

Always remember that all feelings are okay. So learn to accept them. Learn to embrace them. They are a part of who you are!

Acknowledge Your Feelings

While exploring a huge theme park, a boy named Andrew got lost. It was getting dark, and he couldn't find his way back to the exit! His parents were nowhere to be seen. He was shaking and trembling, and his heart was beating fast. Luckily, a park attendant saw him and helped him.

Did he feel terrified? You bet! Fear can make some kids shy away from trying out new things or from going to new places.

Andrew recognized the feeling of being scared. After calming himself down, he decided he would be more alert and careful in public places. But it doesn't mean that he would stop going to theme parks and having fun.

Meanwhile, Dana notices the snickers and whispers of her schoolmates because she wore her thick glasses to school for the first time. Some of the kids made fun of her at lunch break. What could she be feeling?

If you guessed angry and frustrated, yes! You're correct. But Dana was able to recognize and acknowledge these emotions. She then realized that lashing out would not do any good. She chose instead to ignore the kids' laughs, knowing that her classmates didn't understand. She said calmly, "Wearing glasses is just like having a cast when your arm is broken. I wear glasses to help me with my vision."

Now let's say your friend Alex got in trouble with his teacher because he was late for school. He felt bad for the rest of the day. You notice that he's not in the mood to play with you or talk to any of his friends even at the end of the day. Do you recognize his feelings? Do you think he's sad or depressed? Or perhaps disappointed at himself?

Yes, all these things could be true. These feelings are normal. But do you think Alex was able to name the feelings and choose what to do with them?

Maybe if thought about his emotions after the teacher scolded him, he would have told himself, "Getting in trouble for being late made me feel bad and sad. But if I get stuck on these feelings, I won't get anything done. So maybe it's better to spend some time with my friends or play soccer at recess so I can start to feel good again. Then next time, I will wake up twenty minutes earlier so I'm not late."

Remember that emotions are just like balls of energy, wanting to find a way to be expressed. They need to get out of you and show themselves. But when you recognize and understand them, you can choose to use them for good. You can express them in a way that will not hurt you or anyone else.

It's important to name your feelings. When you know what they are, it will be easier to manage them or control them.

. . .

How to Deal with Feeling Angry

"Gggrrrrr!!! Aaaarrrrggghhhh!!!!"

"I hate you!!!!"

Have you ever yelled at someone or thrown a tantrum because you were so angry? Have you ever said hateful and painful words because you were so mad?

Some people hit things, scream, or yell when they get angry. Others turn red, stomp their feet, slam the door, or clench their teeth.

ANGER RULES

IT IS OK TO GET MAD, BUT...

DON'T HURT OTHERS
DON'T HURT YOURSELF
DON'T DESTROY PROPERTY

WHAT ARE SOME THINGS YOU CAN DO INSTEAD?

1. _____

2. _____

3. _____

4. _____

Anger is a feeling that we all experience from time to time. It's a big, powerful emotion that bubbles up when we're upset, frustrated, or hurt by something or someone.

But hey, feeling angry doesn't make you a bad person! It's totally okay to feel mad sometimes. However, it's important to remember that it's not okay to hurt yourself or others when you're feeling this way. We should never break or destroy things when we're angry.

Anger is a normal emotion, and the key is to find healthy ways to express it. You must find a special way to let out all that strong energy without hurting anything or anyone.

What's important is that you remain in charge. You stay in control. You have the power to handle your anger in a good way. One way to do this is to figure out your "anger triggers" and explore ways to deal with them.

When was the last time you got angry? Can you remember why?

What are the things that make you feel mad?

An anger trigger is like a special button that can set off your anger. It's something that happens or something someone says that makes you react in a certain way.

THINGS THAT MAKE ME FEEL
ANGRY!

It's interesting to know that everyone has their unique anger triggers. Yours may be different from the anger triggers of your siblings or your best friend.

For example, you may feel angry when you're treated unfairly, while others may get angry when they feel like nobody's listening to them. There are lots of different reasons why someone might feel angry. You need to understand your reasons.

Did you know that you can stop some triggers or keep them away? Yup, that's right! Pretty cool, huh?

For example, let's say being tired makes you angry. Well, that means you need to stay away from stressful and tiring activities. Getting enough rest is super important too! You can also be smart in managing your time to prevent getting really tired. For example, you could do your homework right after school so you don't stay up late finishing it.

However, there are also things that we can't always avoid. Like when some people treat you unfairly or bully you. Those are things you can't change because someone else is in control of doing them. But you know what? You can learn how to cope when someone does these things.

Coping means finding healthy ways to deal with difficult situations. Some kids cope with anger by squeezing a ball or writing a letter. Others find joy in singing, dancing, doing physical activities, or even practicing breathing exercises.

What relaxes you and makes you smile? What makes you calm down when you're angry? Maybe it's talking to a person you like and trust. Or perhaps it's doing jumping jacks or running around. Maybe you'll count from 1 to 10, then take a few deep breaths. And hey, listening to your favorite music might just be your secret relaxation weapon!

Remember that different people have different ways of coping. You don't have to follow the examples above exactly. You can create your own unique strategies that work best for you!

How to Deal with Feeling Sad

When was the last time you felt a little down and wished you could chase those gloomy clouds away?

Well, guess what? Some awesome tricks can help turn that frown into a big, happy grin!

When you're feeling sad, you may notice you slump your shoulders and just want to be alone. You may feel tired or sleepy. Things you usually enjoy don't seem as exciting anymore.

These are just some signs of sadness. But remember, everyone feels it differently.

Feeling sad is totally okay. It's a normal and healthy way of feeling when unhappy things happen in life.

But here's the cool part — you have the power to do something about it! That feeling won't stick around forever. You can share your emotions with someone you trust or try doing things that make you feel better.

Would you like to keep feeling sad? Nah, I didn't think so!

Feeling happy and fantastic is definitely much more awesome!

Pretend your sadness is a broken toy. You can use two types of special tools to fix it. The first type of tool is what we call "calming friends".

Calming Friend #1: Mr. Name-That-Feeling

Mr. Name-That-Feeling can calm you down by making you understand what you're feeling. He's gonna make you say, "I'm feeling sad because my brother broke my robot car." Or say, "I'm feeling disappointed because my mom didn't say 'Good job' when I got an A in school."

Calming Friend #2: Ms. Comforter

Ms. Comforter will tell you, "Go share your feelings with someone you trust, such as your mom or your best friend!" Even a short talk and a hug can help you get rid of the gloomies and clear your mind.

The second type of fixing tool is known as a "joy booster".

Joy Booster #1: The Do-What-You-Love Formula

What makes your heart go "Woohoo!!!"? Is it drawing, dancing, listening to your favorite songs, or playing a game? Anything that you love to do, just do it! It'll bring a smile to your face in no time!

Joy Booster #2: The Happy Thoughts Button

Click that secret button in your head, the one that makes you remember the good things you have and the happy memories that made you smile and squeal and jump up and down!

Has your cousin made you laugh so hard that you couldn't stop? Remember that moment! Did you go to Disneyland with your family and have a blast riding all the rides? Think of that great day!

See? There are several "calming friends" and "joy boosters" that you can use when you're feeling sad.

As you go through life, you'll add more "calming friends" and "joy boosters" to your collection of special tools. You'll become an expert at making yourself feel happier and finding peace whenever you need it!

RISE AND SHINE WITH CONFIDENCE

Boom-boom-boom. What's that noise? It's your heart pounding! Your palms are sweaty, and your hands are shaking. Then you feel butterflies fluttering in your stomach.

Have you ever felt this way?

It's what happens when you're nervous or scared. Sometimes, we face challenges and go through experiences that cause this feeling.

Maybe it's your first time speaking in front of the class or performing on stage. Perhaps you're taking an important test or are at a party where you don't know anyone.

These things can give you the heebie-jeebies!

But guess what? That's totally normal. A lot of kids go through the same thing. And yes, even adults do too! Remember, you're a superhero inside, and you need to let that hero shine.

Feeling nervous is a sign that you may feel unsure about the situation. You still need to work on bringing out that "Confidence Superpower" that you have within you.

This is the perfect opportunity to build your confidence!

Unlocking Your Confidence Superpower

Whoa! Confidence is such a big word. But what does it mean?

It's the ability to say, "I can do it!" instead of "I can't do it." It means you trust yourself, and you believe that you are strong and mighty.

You've used confidence if you've learned to ride a bike. On a bike, you move forward smoothly as you pedal. Even if you sometimes wobble or fall, confidence helps you get back up and try again. It makes you keep going!

Confidence is a SUPERPOWER that you can unlock within you!

Like other superheroes, you have missions. Here are four important missions for you to finish to unlock your "Confidence Superpower":

Mission #1: Know your skills and talents, and make them shine.

Think of the praises you've received in the past. Did someone tell you that you look fantastic? Did someone tell you that you made a funny joke? Have you ever heard someone say you're great at sports, art, or writing?

Write down all of these amazing things that people said about you before. Then add the things that you know you're good at.

Now read your list. Does it remind you that you're spectacular and special in your own way? Does it make you feel more confident about taking on new things and challenges in your life?

Reminding yourself about your positive traits and the things you're good at can boost your confidence. Celebrate them! Make them shine even more!

If you have a great imagination and you're fantastic at being creative, then share those splendid stories you wrote, comic books you drew, or special designs you made. You can join art clubs and contests. Put on a puppet show. Explore museums. This way, you can embrace your talent. It will make you feel wonderful!

If you're good at science, how about entering the science fair or starting a science project at school? If you don't know your talent yet, volunteer! Go help someone and try out new things.

Mission #2: Use positive and encouraging words when talking to yourself.

Imagine you're playing a game. You collect gold to beat the negative monster inside your brain!

Every time you say, "I can't!", you lose a gold piece. But you get another one every time you say "I can!".

So go ahead and think of all the "I can..." statements for yourself — every single day! Make it a habit and see the difference it makes in your life!

The next time you get up on stage for a performance, tell yourself, "I can do this. I've practiced many times, and I am prepared. I can share my talent and make people happy."

The next time you play soccer or basketball, tell yourself, "I can help my team in this game. I can use the skills I learned. I can have fun."

Remember the inner cheerleader that we talked about before? It's always there within you.

Imagine that cheerleader shouting, "Rah! Rah! Rah! I can do it! Go, go, go!"

Use this cheerleader to make you more confident. Choose positive words for yourself all the time.

Mission #3: Set goals and push yourself.

Imagine you are at the starting line of a race track. You crouch down, waiting for the go signal. You look ahead, ready to start running because you can't wait to reach the finish line.

In this example, the goal is to get to the finish line. If there is no goal, you might just sit down and never move at all!

What are goals? These are the things you would like to achieve or to have for yourself.

Maybe you have a goal to become a better athlete. Maybe you want to get a medal in school.

Goals can be something you can get in just a small bit of time or a very long time.

For example, your goal for this week may be to wake up early and never be late for school again. But your goal for the next five years might be to become one of the best dancers in town.

Once you achieve a goal, always try for something bigger and better. Take it one step at a time.

You can push or challenge yourself to go for something more.

For example, if you wanted to join a dance team and you already did that, maybe next year you can challenge yourself to win a dance competition.

Or maybe your first goal was to make a new friend this week and you already did that. The next step could be to help those friends with something like schoolwork or basketball.

Set goals that can really be done. You can start small and grow from there. Don't forget to celebrate the little wins along the way!

Mission #4: Try and learn new things.

Curious about swimming, but kinda scared of the water? Or maybe you want to dance, but you're feeling shy?

You know, sometimes trying new things can be pretty tough, especially if we've never done them before. We might be worried about not knowing what to do. But don't worry! We can turn those worries around.

Let's say you're afraid of water. Instead of letting that fear hold you back, how about turning it into a challenge? You can say to yourself, "I'm going to learn how to swim so I can conquer this fear and feel confident in the water!"

And if you're feeling a bit shy about dancing, that's totally okay too! Instead of letting shyness stop you from showing off your awesome dance moves, why not make it a mission to break out of your shell? Tell yourself, "I'm going to learn how to dance so I can let my inner superstar shine and have a blast!"

Remember, trying something new can be a little scary at first, but it can also be a fantastic adventure! So yeah, be brave and give it a shot! You'll see. It's going to be super fun too.

Have you ever tried catching a fish? Have you ever made a painting on a canvas? Have you ever baked cupcakes? These are some of the new things you can try and learn.

After learning something new, it gives you that awesome feeling. You can tell yourself, "I did it!" You'll suddenly feel like smiling and dancing! And that's when confidence grows again.

When you do these missions, it is like you are watering a confidence seed inside yourself. Each mission makes it grow taller and bigger.

Soon you will get to unlock that "Confidence Superpower"!

5

THINK BIG, GROW BIGGER

Have you ever heard of the super popular story called "The Tortoise and the Hare"? It's all about a speedy hare and a slow but determined tortoise.

In the story, the hare thinks he's the fastest thing around and gets a bit too full of himself. He starts goofing off, playing games, and taking long naps instead of focusing on the race. He does this because he is so sure he will win against a tortoise.

Meanwhile, the tortoise thinks, "I may be slow, but I'm steady as can be!" He keeps crawling along. He never gives up. One step at a time, he reaches the end. And guess what? He actually ends up winning the race!

You know, even if you're not the fastest or the best at something right now, just like our turtle friend, it doesn't mean you can't succeed.

It's not about being born with talent or skill. Nope, it's not about luck, either. It's all about having something called a "growth mindset." If you have a growth mindset, you believe in yourself. You believe you can learn and improve when you set your mind to something.

Wait. We're saying you don't need talent to do something? Yup! Anyone can get better and still come out on top. So keep going, keep growing, and remember, slow and steady wins the race!

. . .

Fixed Mindset vs. Growth Mindset

Picture your brain as a mysterious world. Inside your brain lives a sneaky villain called Fixed Mindset. This guy loves to play tricks and mess around with your thoughts. He's always whispering things like:

"You're not talented."

"You're not as good as that other kid."

"You're not a math person. That's why you get bad grades in math."

"You can't learn that because you're not smart enough."

Do you sometimes hear these words in your head? It's that pesky Fixed Mindset whispering them! Fixed Mindset likes to keep you stuck and make you believe that you cannot improve, even when you can. This villain makes you give up easily. He keeps you from trying new things because he's afraid of failure. Get ready to put on your superhero cape. You gotta stop this villain from messing with your head!

Luckily, your brain is also home to a mighty superhero sidekick called Growth Mindset. She's the one that shouts at the top of her lungs, "You can do it if you try!" and "Mistakes help you learn and get better!"

This superhero believes that you can get better at anything with effort and practice. The growth mindset helps you love new experiences. She encourages you to believe in yourself and to keep on learning.

And here's the thing. Together, you and Growth Mindset can defeat that villain, Fixed Mindset. And when you do this, you'll be surprised at the amazing adventures you can have!

With a growth mindset, you'll get to be the ultimate, super-duper version of yourself!

Help Growth Mindset Win!

Let's get to it. How exactly can you give the superhero Growth Mindset a boost inside your brain?

First of all, believe in yourself. You have incredible powers inside of you!

Notice when Fixed Mindset whispers in your brain. Whenever he sneaks into your thoughts and says you can't do something, shout back. Tell him, "I can do anything if I try!"

Do you remember when we talked about the power of the word "yet"? Pull out that superpower now! When you're discouraged and you feel like you can't do something, try putting the word "yet" at the end.

"I don't know how to cook spaghetti. . . yet."

"I'm not good at bowling . . . yet."

"I can't make new friends . . . yet."

Second, keep in mind that mistakes are magical. They are your secret weapons for growth.

You can use mistakes to get better at something. Every time you make a boo-boo, smile and know that it's all good. A mistake means that you tried. It also means that you can do things differently next time.

Third, remember that challenges are your buddies! They are not monsters to run away from. Instead, give those challenges a high-five. Tell them, "Bring it on!" They can make you braver, stronger, and smarter.

Fourth, collect positive (nice) words in your head. Each time you try something hard, fight the negative thoughts with positive words. Tell yourself, "I'm making progress" instead of saying, "I'm failing again." Tell yourself, "I can figure this out!" instead of saying "I'm doomed!"

And lastly, hang out with friends who make you feel good. These are the friends who cheer you on and say, "Hey, you've got this!"

They can make a huge difference.

Make Growth Mindset win in your head! It can do wonders for you!

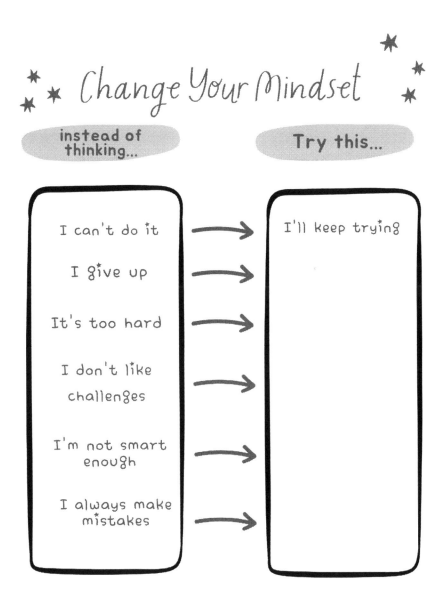

GROWTH MINDSET

Change your mindset- change your life

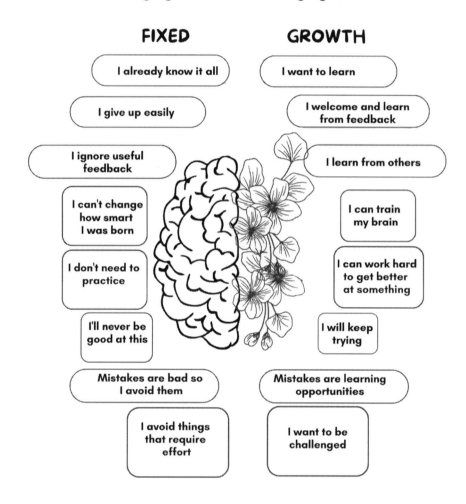

FIXED

GROWTH

I already know it all

I want to learn

I give up easily

I welcome and learn from feedback

I ignore useful feedback

I learn from others

I can't change how smart I was born

I can train my brain

I don't need to practice

I can work hard to get better at something

I'll never be good at this

I will keep trying

Mistakes are bad so I avoid them

Mistakes are learning opportunities

I avoid things that require effort

I want to be challenged

6

FRIENDSHIP EXPLORER'S HANDBOOK

D id you know that animals can have friends too? It's true!

It's not just humans who have buddies. Isn't that amazing? Scientists have discovered that creatures like elephants, dolphins, horses, baboons, and whales can have pals just like us!

Believe it or not, animal friends help each other out. They watch each other's backs and share food and homes. Sometimes, they even team up to catch their dinner or protect themselves from scary enemies. Animals know that friendships are important for their happiness and survival.

Now let's talk about what makes a strong friendship. It all starts with communication and spending time together. How often do you chat with your friends? Do you share your exciting ideas and goals with them? And do you listen carefully when they tell you how they're feeling?

If you answered "yes" to all these questions, then you're on the right track to having awesome friendships! You see, good communication is the secret to building great relationships.

Making Friends

When Max started a new school, he felt nervous and worried about making friends. Have you felt like this before?

It can be tough! In the beginning, Max sat alone at lunch and played by himself on the playground. He tried to be brave and was determined to find some great pals.

One day, Max saw a girl named Elise playing soccer. He asked if he could join her. She quickly smiled and said, "Sure! The more, the merrier!"

Just like Max, you can definitely make new friends! Walk up to someone at school and say something friendly. You can join a game with them or ask questions like, "What's your favorite hobby?" or "Do you have a pet at home?" Showing you want to get to know them is a fantastic way to start a chat!

If you have a chance to show kindness, do it! That might mean helping someone carry their books or sharing your food with them. These are great ways to start a friendship too! And of course, never forget to smile and brighten someone's day!

As Max and Elise played together, they discovered they had a lot in common. They both loved mystery stories and chocolate ice cream. They laughed and had so much fun during recess. Who would have thought, right?

From that day forward, they became the best of friends. They ate lunch together and helped one another. Max learned that friends encourage each other to be their best. He became more confident because Elise always believed in him.

Max also discovered that it's okay to disagree at times because friendship isn't about doing everything together always. He learned to listen, be understanding, and find solutions that made them both happy. They respected each other and understood the power of teamwork. They realized that together they could accomplish marvelous things!

So here's a super fun challenge for you this week: Make a new friend! Get to know each other and do some cool things together. Have fun!

How to Be a Good Friend

Woohoo! Now that you've got yourself some awesome friends, just like Max, it's time to think about how you can become the BEST EVER buddy to them!

First of all, you've got to be their personal cheerleader, always ready to wave your pompoms for them. Do we mean real pompoms? Nope (but those are cool too, if you have them!). When Max missed a soccer goal, Elise cheered him up. That's what a cheerleader does! And when Elise won a story-writing contest, Max was the first one to tell her she did a great job.

Be that pal people can count on. Listen when they're sharing their feelings and dreams or just talking about what happened that day.

Next, just let your heart shine. Show that you care about those important moments. When Max got the highest quiz score in the class, who was the first to clap? Elise! And when Elise put on a bake sale? Max was there to help her prepare the goodies and spread the word about it!

Also make sure to treat friends with respect all the time, even when you don't agree on something. Always be kind and sensitive to their feelings.

What else do you need to know about friendships? It's important to always speak the truth, even when it's difficult. This is a great way to build trust in your friendship. Believe me, your friends will appreciate it.

And if you ever mess up, be willing to say sorry. When Max hurt Elise's feelings by accident, he apologized, and she realized he made a mistake. The pain went away, and their friendship became stronger!

Finally, know that it's okay to be different from your friends. You can be friends with those who are very different from you. Isn't it more fun when you get all sorts of gifts on your birthday? Your friends are like those gifts. They're all nice and special in their unique ways.

Max and Elise made other friends too — kids who loved watching movies instead of reading stories and classmates who liked french fries more than ice cream! That's okay! They still loved hanging out together.

. . .

Handling Jealousy

Psst! Have you ever gotten jealous when your pal started hanging out with someone new? Hey, it's fine! No need to hide it.

Jealousy is a totally normal feeling that can happen to any of us. It's just a sign that you care about your friendship and worry it might change because of someone or something else.

When you feel jealous, try talking about your feelings with your friend using your super polite words. Don't forget to be your own cheerleader too! Instead of moping and thinking, "Why doesn't my friend want to hang out with me anymore? Am I not cool enough?" think positive thoughts. Remind yourself of all the fantastic reasons you two became friends and the incredible adventures you've shared.

Now, what if your friend is the one that's jealous because you've made a new buddy? Fear not! Try saying something nice like, "Hey, I'm sorry if you felt left out, but you mean the world to me. Let's all hang out together!" This way, your friend will know they're still special in your life. They'll learn making new buddies doesn't mean leaving old ones behind.

Here's another sticky situation you might find yourself in. Your friend feels jealous when you ace a test and they don't. Yikes! In this case, swoop in and say, "Hey, we both rocked it, and that's what matters, right? Come on, let's celebrate both our scores!"

Remember, the words you speak and the actions you take hold real power! So open up and talk to your friend when jealousy pays you a visit. Together, you can overcome any bout of jealousy and make your friendship even stronger.

Communication is key, and it doesn't always mean talking. Even writing letters or giving a friendly pat on the back can work wonders! Sometimes, a big ole hug or doing something kind for your friend can say a lot without any words at all.

Remember, when you express yourself, it shows how much you care and can make a world of difference in your friendship. So, let those words flow, and let your actions show that you've got your friend's back!

7

SUPERPOWER HABITS

I magine this. You wake up one day and discover you've got an incredible superpower! How cool would that be? What would you do with your new ability?

Would you use your powers to take down bad villains and lend a helping hand to those in need? Or would you fly through the sky or become invisible at will? There are so many possibilities.

Now here's a little secret: You may not have the ability to fly (bummer, I know), but don't worry! I've got something even better to share with you — the secret to becoming a super awesome kid with superpower habits!

While you may not have the ability to shoot lasers from your eyes, you can still gain incredible habits that make you shine like a true superhero. Want to learn more? Trust me, it's going to blow your mind!

. . .

Getting Enough Sleep

I know your regular day is busy. You go to school, take care of your cat or dog, hang out with friends, practice sports, and do homework. Phew, that's a lot!

Your body needs a break. And that's where sleep swoops in to save the day. It's like giving your body a power-packed recharge!

Think about it. Sleep isn't just for humans like you and me. Notice how your furry pals cozy up for their own little nap sessions. Cats and dogs sleep too to give their bodies a mini-vacation. We all need sleep to have enough energy for the next day!

Kids ages 5 to 12 should get 9 to 12 hours of sleep each night. But remember, everyone's different. Some kids might need a little more sleep than others.

Think back to a time when you didn't get enough sleep. That felt awful, right? And let me tell you, when you're running on empty, you're not doing your best. Too little sleep can bring out your moody, tired, and cranky sides. We don't want that! You'll have a hard time paying attention or following directions. Even easy schoolwork can feel impossible. You could even have trouble playing your favorite sport or musical instrument.

Oh, and here's another thing. Getting enough sleep isn't just about feeling your best. It will help you grow and fight off sickness. Good sleep can help keep those pesky colds away. So yes, snoozing isn't just for re-energizing. It's a secret ingredient for healthy growth too!

Sleep is a superpower habit that'll make you enjoy life a whole lot more! Give your body the rest it craves and watch as you become a well-rested superhero, ready to conquer each day.

Eating Well

Do you love eating pizza, burgers, and chips? What about munching on cookies and cakes?

Uh-oh, watch out! These are troublemakers known as junk food. They may cause you to lose your powers.

Candy and soda might be delicious, but they can harm your teeth and leave you feeling sleepy. Have just a little bit of these treats while also drinking 6 to 8 glasses of water every day.

Healthy eating is all about mixing it up! Put different types of food in every meal. Throw in some fruits or veggies with your meat! Try some oatmeal for breakfast.

Here's a fun tip that all you artsy kids will love. Make your plates colorful! Think orange carrots and red apples with your white chicken! Or a green salad with yellow cheese next to a delicious brown porkchop. These foods are like a team of superheroes, each with its own powers to keep you healthy and strong.

Eating healthily fuels you so you can grow and think clearly all the time. Healthy food gives you a burst of energy. It also boosts those sickness fighters within your body!

And did you know that healthy food powers up the brain too? It helps your mind work better so you can feel smarter and more creative.

Eat snacks and meals that are good for your body, and you'll be surprised at all the amazing things you can do!

D oing Physical Activity

Your army of healthy buddies doesn't just include sleep and healthy eating. Meet the third member of the team — physical activity!

Go ahead and move, move, move!

You can exercise with jumping jacks and jogging. You can also have fun playing basketball and volleyball with your friends. You can even run around with your pet or bike to school. These fun things are so good for your body!

Do you love to dance? That's another fun way to get your heart pumping and make your body fit and healthy.

Exercise doesn't have to be boring. There are lots of physical activities that you can do by yourself or with others!

Play tag or slide on the playground. Maybe you just help a parent with sweeping the floor. These are all great ways to get the daily exercise your body needs.

When you're exercising, your heart starts pumping, and your muscles get stronger with each move you make. It's like a happy dance party is going on inside you!

After physical activity, something magical happens. It's like you get a burst of oxygen in your mind and body, and you feel incredible!

Physical activities are like little happiness boosters. So make it a superpower habit and keep your body healthy with a big smile on your face!

Reading

Imagine if you can get transported to different worlds through a portal! Would you choose to travel through space, explore a jungle, or go back in time to visit an ancient civilization? All these are possible — within the pages of a book!

Yes, reading can take you from one adventure to another! Every book you open is a new quest. It's a chance to discover mind-blowing facts or experience a place you've never been to.

And did you know that reading is like a secret code to a world of words? Reading can help you become a word master. That means you can talk about your ideas like never before!

Oh, and here's a little secret trick. Try your hand at writing, and watch your imagination run wild! You can create beautiful stories that readers far and wide love.

Need awesome tips to make your reading journey even more epic?

Tip #1: Find books that make your curiosity burst like a volcano! Choose topics you love and make you go, "Wow, I must know more!"

Tip #2: Challenge yourself with reading goals. A good goal is finishing one book per week. Soon you'll be a champion of books!

Are you ready to become a legendary reading superhero? Your brain is going to fly to new heights, and it'll thank you!

8

MAGICAL MANNERS

D id you know that shaking hands has a super cool origin story?

Hundreds of years ago in England, people started shaking hands to show that they came in peace. Shaking hands showed people they did not have any weapons hidden up their sleeves. It was like a secret code that said, "Hey, I'm friendly! I won't hurt you!"

Today, shaking hands is one way of showing good manners when meeting someone new.

Here's another fun fact! A long, long time ago, some people believed that yawning was the soul trying to escape the body. Others believed it was evil spirits sneaking inside! Scary or weird? Probably both! This is why many started to cover their mouths when they yawned.

And now, we do this to show good manners. Some people think it's rude to show that you're yawning.

What Good Manners Mean

What are good manners, anyway?

Well, they're like a special charm that brings kindness, happiness, and respect to everyone around you. They are actions or words that show people you care about them.

And what's even more exciting is that they can make you and others feel awesome!

Basic Manners to Learn

Picture this: Your mom's angry because you haven't cleaned your room for a week, and you're about to go to the park.

Mom: Can you please clean your room before going out to play? You promised to do it yesterday. And the day before that too.

You: I'm so sorry, Mom. I'll do it right away.

[After one hour...]

You: It's a big mess! It'll take me forever!

You peek outside and see your sister reading a book.

You: Excuse me. Is it okay if I ask you for help?

Sister: (puts down her book) Sure. What's wrong?

You: Can you please help me clean my room? You're really good at being neat and tidy.

Sister: Okay, no problem.

After another hour...

You: (happy) Wow, it's finally done! It doesn't look like a zoo anymore.

Sister: And it doesn't smell like a zoo either!

You: (laughing and hugging your sister) Thank you so much!

Sister: You're welcome.

You: Come on, let's show Mom. Then you can play with me and my friends at the park.

Sister: Okay! We make a great team!

Play Treasure Hunt and search for these four magical phrases in the conversation above: Please, Thank You, Excuse Me, and I'm Sorry.

Why are they important?

Saying "please" is a magical way to show thoughtfulness. That's another big word! It means you're thinking about the feelings of another person. It's like spreading kindness in the air!

When you say "thank you", you're showing how grateful you are for what someone did for you or gave to you. It's a great way to appreciate the gift or act of kindness.

"Excuse me" is a magical phrase that makes the world more polite. It's a way to ask for forgiveness or get someone's attention in a good way.

And finally, saying "I'm sorry" can help heal broken hearts and hurt feelings. You can show you care after making a mistake with your words or actions.

General Good Manners

It's Saturday! You wake up all excited to go to your cousin's house with your best friend.

You: Let's go, Billy! I'm excited to play at Kyle's house! He said he will show us this super cool treehouse that Uncle John built in their backyard.

Billy: But isn't it too early to go?

You: It's okay. I'm sure he's already awake.

At Kyle's house, You and Billy knock gently on the door. Knocking on someone's door instead of just going inside is like saying, "Excuse me, may I come in?" It's a good way to show respect.

Your Uncle John opens the door and smiles.

Uncle John: Oh, hi, guys! Welcome! Come in and sit down I'll go get Kyle.

Greeting guests is another way to show good manners. Make them feel welcome in your home.

You: Thanks so much, Uncle John!

You open the door and hold it while Billy walks in. This is another way to show respect for someone.

While waiting for Kyle to come, you suddenly feel a sneeze coming! You cover your nose and mouth with a tissue. It's the polite way to avoid spreading germs.

Finally, Kyle comes out. He looks excited.

Kyle: Wow, you guys are early! That's awesome. We can play longer in the treehouse!

He leads you to the backyard and shows you his big, beautiful treehouse.

Billy: Wow, it's so cool! Your father is great at building! Thanks so much for having us over.

You: You painted it, right? And I can see that you even added some drawings on the side! Cool! You're such a good artist!

Kyle: Thank you. Dad and I did a great job, and we're going to have the time of our lives!

Giving a compliment or words of praise is like sending boosts of happiness that make people feel good. Saying someone is a good builder or a talented artist is an example of a compliment.

Kyle: Come on, let's climb up!

The three of you rush forward, but only one person at a time can use the steps. You wait for your turn instead of pushing. Waiting is a cool way to give everyone a chance to have fun!

Up in the treehouse, you share Kyle's toys and play some games. You almost lose track of time because you're having so much fun! You find some paper and markers to write a thank-you note to Kyle and his dad.

You: Thanks so much for this awesome day, Kyle!

Kyle: You're welcome! But hey, it's not over yet. Mom's making lunch for us.

You: Wow, I can't wait!

Billy: And after lunch, we're still going to ride our bikes outside, right?

Kyle: Oh, yeah!

You clean up the toys you played with before going inside. Aunt Alice is done cooking your lunch, and it smells so delicious! You offer to set the table, and she's very grateful.

Aunt Alice: You are such nice kids. Thanks for helping out!

Uncle John: Grab a seat, and let's eat!

Helping cheers up people. There are many small deeds we can do for others that can make a huge difference.

After eating, you clean up after yourself. It's another way to show good manners and to say thank you to your host.

A Little More to Remember

Now it's time to learn the art of table manners! Here are two important rules to make mealtime fun:

First, remember to keep your mouth closed when you chew, like a sneaky squirrel with a secret stash of acorns. No one wants to see food flying out while you're talking! Take small bites and enjoy the flavor. When you're ready to speak, politely swallow before sharing your amazing stories.

Second, let's turn off those electronics for a bit! Give your full attention to the delicious meal and awesome company at the table. This is a great time to chat with family and friends!

Practicing good table manners makes mealtimes extra special. Bon appétit and let the fun begin!

Now, you're ready to become a master of good manners!

It doesn't matter if it's morning, noon, or night. Anytime is perfect to show your thoughtful and polite side. And guess what? The secret to starting is as simple as a smile!

Then with time and practice, you can learn more good manners. Be patient with yourself. Always remember, the golden rule of manners is treating others the way you want to be treated. Makes perfect sense, right?

You can be an even greater version of yourself when you're always showing good manners. People will absolutely love you, and you'll feel marvelous!

CONCLUSION

Congratulations, remarkable readers! You've just completed this thrilling adventure of self-discovery and growth! You've discovered skills you're capable of that you didn't know existed within you. You've set free that mighty superhero inside you!

Remember, becoming the most awesome version of yourself isn't a destination — it's a journey you'll always be on. But now you know there are no limits to what you can achieve. When you look in the mirror, you'll now see a lion instead of a cat. You'll proudly say, "You're a champ!" instead of "You're a loser."

You've learned to think positively, and your confidence has grown. You know how to use that growth mindset so it can push you forward during challenging times.

But that's not all! You've learned how to be an amazing friend, show respect and be polite through good manners, develop healthy habits, and yes, even how to handle money! Wow!

So as this adventure comes to an end, always remember the gigantic potential that lives within you. You're capable of shining brightly like the rarest diamond!

Take these lessons and newfound superpowers with you, and never give up. Be happy and go for all of your dreams. This is only the beginning of your incredible journey to becoming the most awesome version of yourself!

Stay super, stay awesome, and keep shining!

HAPPY KIDS' HANDBOOK

Hey, fellow bookworms! 👋 Welcome to our fun and fantastic Book Review Club. 📖

You love reading, right? 📖 Well, us too! And the best part about finishing a cool book is talking about it with friends. So, let's do that right here, in our super-duper Book Review Club!

What's Your Favorite Part of the Story?

Did anything in the book make you laugh or feel excited? Tell us your favorite part without giving away the ending!

If you had to tell your friend if they should read this book, what would you say? You can even give the book a star rating, like 1 star ⭐ (I didn't like it) up to 5 stars ⭐⭐⭐⭐⭐ (I loved it)!

And that's it! You've written a book review. 🎉 Isn't that fun? Remember, you're not only sharing your thoughts but also helping your friends discover awesome books.

(PS: Parents, don't forget to help your little ones type their reviews if they need it. Together, we're growing readers every day! 🌱)

REFERENCES

All for KIDZ, Inc. (2014). How Full is Your Bucket? For Kids Lesson Plan. Retrieved from http://thenedshow.com/assets/encourage-others-intermediate-lesson-plan-how-full-is-your-bucket.pdf

Ana Life Coach: Growing Resilience Kids & Teens. (n.d). Ideas on How to Help Children Stop Comparing with Others. Retrieved from https://growingresilienceinkids.com/ideas-on-how-to-help-children-stop-comparing-with-others/

The Behavior Hub. (2020, March). Children's Emotions: How They Work and Behavior Strategies to Try. Retrieved from https://www.thebehaviorhub.com/blog/2020/4/9/childrens-emotions

The Center on the Social and Emotional Foundations for Early Learning. (n.d). Teaching Your Child to Identify and Express

Emotions. Retrieved from http://csefel.vanderbilt.edu/familytools/teaching_emotions.pdf

Goddard-Hill, Becky. (2021, June). How to Teach Kids Self-Kindness. Retrieved from https://happiful.com/how-to-teach-kids-self-kindness

Millacci, Tiffany Sauber Ph.D. (2021, December). How to Nurture a Growth Mindset in Kids: 8 Best Acivities. Retrieved from https://positivepsychology.com/growth-mindset-for-kids/#:~:text=References-,Growth%20vs%20Fixed%20Mindset%3A%20Definition%20for%20Kids,you%20cannot%20learn%20new%20things.

The Prindle Institute for Ethics. (n.d). The Ugly Duckling: Book Module. Retrieved from https://www.prindleinstitute.org/books/the-ugly-duckling/

The Random Acts of Kindness Foundation. (n.d). How Full is Your Bucket? Retrieved from https://www.redlandsusd.net/cms/lib/CA01900901/Centricity/Domain/4821/K_caring_-for_others_how_full_is_your_bucket.pdf

Vamdatt, Rishi. (n.d). Comparison: Stocks vs. Bonds for Kids and Beginners — A Simple Comparison. Retrieved from https://www.easypeasyfinance.com/stocks-vs-bonds-comparison-for-kids/

Made in the USA
Las Vegas, NV
01 November 2023

80017248R00055